Send *Blessings Above*
Gratitude Journal

Gratitude Journal Christian

ACTIVINOTES

Activinotes

DAILY JOURNALS, PLANNERS, NOTEBOOKS AND OTHER BLANK BOOKS

This Book Belongs To

_____

Day: _____ Date: _____

The weather today:

_____
_____
_____

Today I feel:

_____
_____
_____
_____

Today I am grateful for:

_____
_____
_____
_____

Inspirations, prayer, scriptures, quotes:

_____
_____
_____
_____

I said a special prayer for:

_____
_____
_____
_____

Prayer(s) answered (comfort, peace, love and miracles)

_____
_____
_____
_____

What I would like to see happen tomorrow (Goals, ideas, etc.)

_____
_____
_____
_____

MY THOUGHTS ✻ FOR THE DAY

Day: _____   Date: _____

The weather today:
_____
_____
_____

Today I feel:
_____
_____
_____

Today I am grateful for:
_____
_____
_____

Inspirations, prayer, scriptures, quotes:
_____
_____
_____

I said a special prayer for:
_____
_____
_____

Prayer(s) answered (comfort, peace, love and miracles)
_____
_____
_____

What I would like to see happen tomorrow (Goals, ideas, etc.)
_____
_____
_____
_____

MY THOUGHTS �֎ FOR THE DAY

Day: _____ Date: _____

The weather today:

_____
_____
_____
_____

Today I feel:

_____
_____
_____
_____

Today I am grateful for:

_____
_____
_____
_____

Inspirations, prayer, scriptures, quotes:

_____
_____
_____
_____

I said a special prayer for:

_____
_____
_____
_____

Prayer(s) answered (comfort, peace, love and miracles)

_____
_____
_____

What I would like to see happen tomorrow (Goals, ideas, etc.)

_____
_____
_____
_____

MY THOUGHTS ✸ FOR THE DAY

Day: _____ Date: _____

The weather today:

_____
_____
_____

Today I feel:

_____
_____
_____
_____

Today I am grateful for:

_____
_____
_____
_____

Inspirations, prayer, scriptures, quotes:

_____
_____
_____
_____

I said a special prayer for:

_____
_____
_____
_____

Prayer(s) answered (comfort, peace, love and miracles)

_____
_____
_____

What I would like to see happen tomorrow (Goals, ideas, etc.)

_____
_____
_____
_____

MY THOUGHTS ✿ FOR THE DAY

Day: _____   Date: _____

The weather today:

_____
_____
_____

Today I feel:

_____
_____
_____

Today I am grateful for:

_____
_____
_____

Inspirations, prayer, scriptures, quotes:

_____
_____
_____

I said a special prayer for:

_____
_____
_____

Prayer(s) answered (comfort, peace, love and miracles)

_____
_____

What I would like to see happen tomorrow (Goals, ideas, etc.)

_____
_____
_____
_____

MY THOUGHTS ✻ FOR THE DAY

Day: _____   *Date:* _____

The weather today:

_____
_____
_____

Today I feel:

_____
_____
_____

Today I am grateful for:

_____
_____
_____

Inspirations, prayer, scriptures, quotes:

_____
_____
_____

I said a special prayer for:

_____
_____
_____

Prayer(s) answered (comfort, peace, love and miracles)

_____
_____
_____

What I would like to see happen tomorrow (Goals, ideas, etc.)

_____
_____
_____
_____

MY THOUGHTS ✳ FOR THE DAY

Day: _____   Date: _____

The weather today:

_____
_____
_____

Today I feel:

_____
_____
_____

Today I am grateful for:

_____
_____
_____

Inspirations, prayer, scriptures, quotes:

_____
_____
_____

I said a special prayer for:

_____
_____
_____

Prayer(s) answered (comfort, peace, love and miracles)

_____
_____
_____

What I would like to see happen tomorrow (Goals, ideas, etc.)

_____
_____
_____
_____

MY THOUGHTS ✤ FOR THE DAY

Day: _____   Date: _____

The weather today:
_____
_____
_____

Today I feel:
_____
_____
_____

Today I am grateful for:
_____
_____
_____

Inspirations, prayer, scriptures, quotes:
_____
_____
_____

I said a special prayer for:
_____
_____
_____

Prayer(s) answered (comfort, peace, love and miracles)
_____
_____
_____

What I would like to see happen tomorrow (Goals, ideas, etc.)
_____
_____
_____
_____

MY THOUGHTS ❋ FOR THE DAY

_____

_____

_____

_____

_____

_____

_____

_____

_____

_____

_____

_____

_____

_____

_____

_____

_____

_____

_____

_____

_____

_____

_____

_____

_____

_____

_____

_____

_____

_____

Day: _____   *Date:* _____

The weather today:

_____

_____

_____

Today I feel:

_____

_____

_____

Today I am grateful for:

_____

_____

_____

Inspirations, prayer, scriptures, quotes:

_____

_____

_____

I said a special prayer for:

_____

_____

_____

Prayer(s) answered (comfort, peace, love and miracles)

_____

_____

_____

What I would like to see happen tomorrow (Goals, ideas, etc.)

_____

_____

_____

_____

MY THOUGHTS ✻ FOR THE DAY

Day: _____   Date: _____

The weather today:

_____
_____
_____

Today I feel:

_____
_____
_____

Today I am grateful for:

_____
_____
_____

Inspirations, prayer, scriptures, quotes:

_____
_____
_____

I said a special prayer for:

_____
_____
_____

Prayer(s) answered (comfort, peace, love and miracles)

_____
_____

What I would like to see happen tomorrow (Goals, ideas, etc.)

_____
_____
_____
_____

MY THOUGHTS ✺ FOR THE DAY

Day: _____   *Date:* _____

The weather today:

_____
_____
_____

Today I feel:

_____
_____
_____
_____

Today I am grateful for:

_____
_____
_____
_____

Inspirations, prayer, scriptures, quotes:

_____
_____
_____
_____

I said a special prayer for:

_____
_____
_____
_____

Prayer(s) answered (comfort, peace, love and miracles)

_____
_____
_____

What I would like to see happen tomorrow (Goals, ideas, etc.)

_____
_____
_____
_____

MY THOUGHTS ❋ FOR THE DAY

_____
_____
_____
_____
_____
_____
_____
_____
_____
_____
_____
_____
_____
_____
_____
_____
_____
_____
_____
_____
_____
_____
_____
_____
_____
_____
_____
_____
_____
_____
_____
_____

Day: _____   *Date:* _____

The weather today:

_____
_____
_____

Today I feel:

_____
_____
_____
_____

Today I am grateful for:

_____
_____
_____
_____

Inspirations, prayer, scriptures, quotes:

_____
_____
_____
_____

I said a special prayer for:

_____
_____
_____
_____

Prayer(s) answered (comfort, peace, love and miracles)

_____
_____
_____

What I would like to see happen tomorrow (Goals, ideas, etc.)

_____
_____
_____
_____

MY THOUGHTS ✳ FOR THE DAY

Day: _____   Date: _____

The weather today:

_____
_____
_____

Today I feel:

_____
_____
_____

Today I am grateful for:

_____
_____
_____

Inspirations, prayer, scriptures, quotes:

_____
_____
_____

I said a special prayer for:

_____
_____
_____

Prayer(s) answered (comfort, peace, love and miracles)

_____
_____
_____

What I would like to see happen tomorrow (Goals, ideas, etc.)

_____
_____
_____
_____

MY THOUGHTS ✻ FOR THE DAY

Day: _____   *Date:* _____

The weather today:

_____

_____

_____

Today I feel:

_____

_____

_____

Today I am grateful for:

_____

_____

_____

Inspirations, prayer, scriptures, quotes:

_____

_____

_____

I said a special prayer for:

_____

_____

_____

Prayer(s) answered (comfort, peace, love and miracles)

_____

_____

_____

What I would like to see happen tomorrow (Goals, ideas, etc.)

_____

_____

_____

_____

MY THOUGHTS ✦ FOR THE DAY

Day: _____   Date: _____

The weather today:
_____
_____
_____

Today I feel:
_____
_____
_____
_____

Today I am grateful for:
_____
_____
_____
_____

Inspirations, prayer, scriptures, quotes:
_____
_____
_____
_____

I said a special prayer for:
_____
_____
_____
_____

Prayer(s) answered (comfort, peace, love and miracles)
_____
_____
_____
_____

What I would like to see happen tomorrow (Goals, ideas, etc.)
_____
_____
_____
_____
_____

MY THOUGHTS ✳ FOR THE DAY

_____

_____

_____

_____

_____

_____

_____

_____

_____

_____

_____

_____

_____

_____

_____

_____

_____

_____

_____

_____

_____

_____

_____

_____

_____

_____

_____

_____

_____

_____

_____

Day: _____   Date: _____

The weather today:

_____
_____
_____

Today I feel:

_____
_____
_____

Today I am grateful for:

_____
_____
_____

Inspirations, prayer, scriptures, quotes:

_____
_____
_____

I said a special prayer for:

_____
_____
_____

Prayer(s) answered (comfort, peace, love and miracles)

_____
_____
_____

What I would like to see happen tomorrow (Goals, ideas, etc.)

_____
_____
_____
_____

MY THOUGHTS ✸ FOR THE DAY

Day: _____   Date: _____

The weather today:

_____
_____
_____

Today I feel:

_____
_____
_____

Today I am grateful for:

_____
_____
_____

Inspirations, prayer, scriptures, quotes:

_____
_____
_____

I said a special prayer for:

_____
_____
_____

Prayer(s) answered (comfort, peace, love and miracles)

_____
_____
_____

What I would like to see happen tomorrow (Goals, ideas, etc.)

_____
_____
_____
_____

MY THOUGHTS FOR THE DAY

Day: _____   Date: _____

The weather today:

_____
_____
_____

Today I feel:

_____
_____
_____

Today I am grateful for:

_____
_____
_____

Inspirations, prayer, scriptures, quotes:

_____
_____
_____

I said a special prayer for:

_____
_____
_____

Prayer(s) answered (comfort, peace, love and miracles)

_____
_____
_____

What I would like to see happen tomorrow (Goals, ideas, etc.)

_____
_____
_____
_____

MY THOUGHTS ✽ FOR THE DAY

_____

_____

_____

_____

_____

_____

_____

_____

_____

_____

_____

_____

_____

_____

_____

_____

_____

_____

_____

_____

_____

_____

_____

_____

_____

_____

_____

_____

_____

Day: _____   Date: _____

The weather today:
_____
_____
_____

Today I feel:
_____
_____
_____
_____

Today I am grateful for:
_____
_____
_____
_____

Inspirations, prayer, scriptures, quotes:
_____
_____
_____
_____

I said a special prayer for:
_____
_____
_____
_____

Prayer(s) answered (comfort, peace, love and miracles)
_____
_____
_____

What I would like to see happen tomorrow (Goals, ideas, etc.)
_____
_____
_____
_____
_____

MY THOUGHTS ✺ FOR THE DAY

Day: _____   Date: _____

The weather today:
_____
_____
_____

Today I feel:
_____
_____
_____
_____

Today I am grateful for:
_____
_____
_____
_____

Inspirations, prayer, scriptures, quotes:
_____
_____
_____
_____

I said a special prayer for:
_____
_____
_____
_____

Prayer(s) answered (comfort, peace, love and miracles)
_____
_____
_____

What I would like to see happen tomorrow (Goals, ideas, etc.)
_____
_____
_____
_____

MY THOUGHTS ✻ FOR THE DAY

_____

_____

_____

_____

_____

_____

_____

_____

_____

_____

_____

_____

_____

_____

_____

_____

_____

_____

_____

_____

_____

_____

_____

_____

_____

_____

_____

Day: _____   Date: _____

The weather today:
_____
_____
_____

Today I feel:
_____
_____
_____
_____

Today I am grateful for:
_____
_____
_____
_____

Inspirations, prayer, scriptures, quotes:
_____
_____
_____
_____

I said a special prayer for:
_____
_____
_____
_____

Prayer(s) answered (comfort, peace, love and miracles)
_____
_____
_____
_____

What I would like to see happen tomorrow (Goals, ideas, etc.)
_____
_____
_____
_____

MY THOUGHTS ❋ FOR THE DAY

Day: _____   *Date:* _____

The weather today:

_____
_____
_____

Today I feel:

_____
_____
_____

Today I am grateful for:

_____
_____
_____

Inspirations, prayer, scriptures, quotes:

_____
_____
_____

I said a special prayer for:

_____
_____
_____

Prayer(s) answered (comfort, peace, love and miracles)

_____
_____
_____

What I would like to see happen tomorrow (Goals, ideas, etc.)

_____
_____
_____
_____

MY THOUGHTS ✸ FOR THE DAY

Day: _____   *Date:* _____

The weather today:

_____
_____
_____

Today I feel:

_____
_____
_____

Today I am grateful for:

_____
_____
_____

Inspirations, prayer, scriptures, quotes:

_____
_____
_____

I said a special prayer for:

_____
_____
_____

Prayer(s) answered (comfort, peace, love and miracles)

_____
_____
_____

What I would like to see happen tomorrow (Goals, ideas, etc.)

_____
_____
_____
_____

MY THOUGHTS �֍ FOR THE DAY

Day: _____   *Date:* _____

The weather today:

_____

_____

_____

Today I feel:

_____

_____

_____

Today I am grateful for:

_____

_____

_____

Inspirations, prayer, scriptures, quotes:

_____

_____

_____

I said a special prayer for:

_____

_____

_____

Prayer(s) answered (comfort, peace, love and miracles)

_____

_____

_____

What I would like to see happen tomorrow (Goals, ideas, etc.)

_____

_____

_____

_____

MY THOUGHTS ✺ FOR THE DAY

_____

_____

_____

_____

_____

_____

_____

_____

_____

_____

_____

_____

_____

_____

_____

_____

_____

_____

_____

_____

_____

_____

_____

_____

_____

_____

_____

_____

_____

Day: _____   *Date:* _____

The weather today:

_____
_____
_____

Today I feel:

_____
_____
_____
_____

Today I am grateful for:

_____
_____
_____
_____

Inspirations, prayer, scriptures, quotes:

_____
_____
_____
_____

I said a special prayer for:

_____
_____
_____
_____

Prayer(s) answered (comfort, peace, love and miracles)

_____
_____
_____

What I would like to see happen tomorrow (Goals, ideas, etc.)

_____
_____
_____
_____
_____

MY THOUGHTS ✻ FOR THE DAY

Day: _____   *Date:* _____

The weather today:

_____
_____
_____

Today I feel:

_____
_____
_____

Today I am grateful for:

_____
_____
_____

Inspirations, prayer, scriptures, quotes:

_____
_____
_____

I said a special prayer for:

_____
_____
_____

Prayer(s) answered (comfort, peace, love and miracles)

_____
_____

What I would like to see happen tomorrow (Goals, ideas, etc.)

_____
_____
_____
_____

MY THOUGHTS �֍ FOR THE DAY

Day: _____ *Date:* _____

The weather today:

_____
_____
_____

Today I feel:

_____
_____
_____

Today I am grateful for:

_____
_____
_____

Inspirations, prayer, scriptures, quotes:

_____
_____
_____

I said a special prayer for:

_____
_____
_____

Prayer(s) answered (comfort, peace, love and miracles)

_____
_____
_____

What I would like to see happen tomorrow (Goals, ideas, etc.)

_____
_____
_____
_____

MY THOUGHTS ✱ FOR THE DAY

_____

_____

_____

_____

_____

_____

_____

_____

_____

_____

_____

_____

_____

_____

_____

_____

_____

_____

_____

_____

_____

_____

_____

_____

_____

_____

_____

_____

_____

_____

_____

Day: _____   Date: _____

The weather today:

_____
_____
_____

Today I feel:

_____
_____
_____
_____

Today I am grateful for:

_____
_____
_____
_____

Inspirations, prayer, scriptures, quotes:

_____
_____
_____
_____

I said a special prayer for:

_____
_____
_____

Prayer(s) answered (comfort, peace, love and miracles)

_____
_____
_____

What I would like to see happen tomorrow (Goals, ideas, etc.)

_____
_____
_____
_____

MY THOUGHTS ✳ FOR THE DAY

_____

_____

_____

_____

_____

_____

_____

_____

_____

_____

_____

_____

_____

_____

_____

_____

_____

_____

_____

_____

_____

_____

_____

_____

_____

_____

_____

_____

_____

_____

_____

_____

Day: _____   Date: _____

The weather today:

_____
_____
_____

Today I feel:

_____
_____
_____

Today I am grateful for:

_____
_____
_____

Inspirations, prayer, scriptures, quotes:

_____
_____
_____

I said a special prayer for:

_____
_____
_____

Prayer(s) answered (comfort, peace, love and miracles)

_____
_____
_____

What I would like to see happen tomorrow (Goals, ideas, etc.)

_____
_____
_____
_____

MY THOUGHTS ✳ FOR THE DAY

Day: _____   *Date:* _____

The weather today:

_____
_____
_____

Today I feel:

_____
_____
_____

Today I am grateful for:

_____
_____
_____

Inspirations, prayer, scriptures, quotes:

_____
_____
_____

I said a special prayer for:

_____
_____
_____

Prayer(s) answered (comfort, peace, love and miracles)

_____
_____
_____

What I would like to see happen tomorrow (Goals, ideas, etc.)

_____
_____
_____

MY THOUGHTS ✳ FOR THE DAY

Day: _____   *Date:* _____

The weather today:
_____
_____
_____

Today I feel:
_____
_____
_____

Today I am grateful for:
_____
_____
_____

Inspirations, prayer, scriptures, quotes:
_____
_____
_____

I said a special prayer for:
_____
_____
_____

Prayer(s) answered (comfort, peace, love and miracles)
_____
_____
_____

What I would like to see happen tomorrow (Goals, ideas, etc.)
_____
_____
_____
_____

MY THOUGHTS ✺ FOR THE DAY

Day: _____   *Date:* _____

The weather today:

_____
_____
_____

Today I feel:

_____
_____
_____
_____

Today I am grateful for:

_____
_____
_____
_____

Inspirations, prayer, scriptures, quotes:

_____
_____
_____
_____

I said a special prayer for:

_____
_____
_____
_____

Prayer(s) answered (comfort, peace, love and miracles)

_____
_____
_____

What I would like to see happen tomorrow (Goals, ideas, etc.)

_____
_____
_____
_____

MY THOUGHTS ✻ FOR THE DAY

Day: _____   Date: _____

The weather today:

_____
_____
_____

Today I feel:

_____
_____
_____
_____

Today I am grateful for:

_____
_____
_____
_____

Inspirations, prayer, scriptures, quotes:

_____
_____
_____
_____

I said a special prayer for:

_____
_____
_____
_____

Prayer(s) answered (comfort, peace, love and miracles)

_____
_____
_____

What I would like to see happen tomorrow (Goals, ideas, etc.)

_____
_____
_____
_____

MY THOUGHTS ✳ FOR THE DAY

Day: _____   Date: _____

The weather today:

_____
_____
_____

Today I feel:

_____
_____
_____

Today I am grateful for:

_____
_____
_____

Inspirations, prayer, scriptures, quotes:

_____
_____
_____

I said a special prayer for:

_____
_____
_____

Prayer(s) answered (comfort, peace, love and miracles)

_____
_____
_____

What I would like to see happen tomorrow (Goals, ideas, etc.)

_____
_____
_____
_____

MY THOUGHTS ✻ FOR THE DAY

Day: _____   Date: _____

The weather today:

_____
_____
_____

Today I feel:

_____
_____
_____

Today I am grateful for:

_____
_____
_____

Inspirations, prayer, scriptures, quotes:

_____
_____
_____

I said a special prayer for:

_____
_____
_____

Prayer(s) answered (comfort, peace, love and miracles)

_____
_____
_____

What I would like to see happen tomorrow (Goals, ideas, etc.)

_____
_____
_____
_____

MY THOUGHTS ✸ FOR THE DAY

Day: _____   *Date:* _____

The weather today:

_____
_____
_____

Today I feel:

_____
_____
_____
_____

Today I am grateful for:

_____
_____
_____
_____

Inspirations, prayer, scriptures, quotes:

_____
_____
_____
_____

I said a special prayer for:

_____
_____
_____
_____

Prayer(s) answered (comfort, peace, love and miracles)

_____
_____
_____
_____

What I would like to see happen tomorrow (Goals, ideas, etc.)

_____
_____
_____
_____
_____

MY THOUGHTS ❋ FOR THE DAY

Day: _____   Date: _____

The weather today:
_____
_____
_____

Today I feel:
_____
_____
_____

Today I am grateful for:
_____
_____
_____

Inspirations, prayer, scriptures, quotes:
_____
_____
_____

I said a special prayer for:
_____
_____
_____

Prayer(s) answered (comfort, peace, love and miracles)
_____
_____
_____

What I would like to see happen tomorrow (Goals, ideas, etc.)
_____
_____
_____
_____

MY THOUGHTS ✺ FOR THE DAY

_____

_____

_____

_____

_____

_____

_____

_____

_____

_____

_____

_____

_____

_____

_____

_____

_____

_____

_____

_____

_____

_____

_____

_____

_____

_____

_____

_____

_____

Day: _____ Date: _____

The weather today:
_____
_____
_____

Today I feel:
_____
_____
_____
_____

Today I am grateful for:
_____
_____
_____
_____

Inspirations, prayer, scriptures, quotes:
_____
_____
_____
_____

I said a special prayer for:
_____
_____
_____
_____

Prayer(s) answered (comfort, peace, love and miracles)
_____
_____
_____
_____

What I would like to see happen tomorrow (Goals, ideas, etc.)
_____
_____
_____
_____

MY THOUGHTS ✻ FOR THE DAY

_____
_____
_____
_____
_____
_____
_____
_____
_____
_____
_____
_____
_____
_____
_____
_____
_____
_____
_____
_____
_____
_____
_____
_____
_____
_____
_____
_____
_____
_____
_____
_____

Day: _____   Date: _____

The weather today:

_____
_____
_____

Today I feel:

_____
_____
_____

Today I am grateful for:

_____
_____
_____

Inspirations, prayer, scriptures, quotes:

_____
_____
_____

I said a special prayer for:

_____
_____
_____

Prayer(s) answered (comfort, peace, love and miracles)

_____
_____
_____

What I would like to see happen tomorrow (Goals, ideas, etc.)

_____
_____
_____
_____

MY THOUGHTS ✺ FOR THE DAY

_____

_____

_____

_____

_____

_____

_____

_____

_____

_____

_____

_____

_____

_____

_____

_____

_____

_____

_____

_____

_____

_____

_____

_____

_____

_____

_____

_____

_____

_____

_____

Day: _____ *Date:* _____

The weather today:

_____

_____

_____

Today I feel:

_____

_____

_____

Today I am grateful for:

_____

_____

_____

Inspirations, prayer, scriptures, quotes:

_____

_____

_____

I said a special prayer for:

_____

_____

_____

Prayer(s) answered (comfort, peace, love and miracles)

_____

_____

_____

What I would like to see happen tomorrow (Goals, ideas, etc.)

_____

_____

_____

_____

MY THOUGHTS ✻ FOR THE DAY

_____
_____
_____
_____
_____
_____
_____
_____
_____
_____
_____
_____
_____
_____
_____
_____
_____
_____
_____
_____
_____
_____
_____
_____
_____
_____
_____
_____
_____
_____

Day: _____   Date: _____

The weather today:
_____
_____
_____

Today I feel:
_____
_____
_____

Today I am grateful for:
_____
_____
_____

Inspirations, prayer, scriptures, quotes:
_____
_____
_____

I said a special prayer for:
_____
_____
_____

Prayer(s) answered (comfort, peace, love and miracles)
_____
_____
_____

What I would like to see happen tomorrow (Goals, ideas, etc.)
_____
_____
_____
_____

MY THOUGHTS �֎ FOR THE DAY

_____

_____

_____

_____

_____

_____

_____

_____

_____

_____

_____

_____

_____

_____

_____

_____

_____

_____

_____

_____

_____

_____

_____

_____

_____

_____

_____

_____

_____

_____

Day: _____   *Date:* _____

The weather today:

_____
_____
_____

Today I feel:

_____
_____
_____
_____

Today I am grateful for:

_____
_____
_____
_____

Inspirations, prayer, scriptures, quotes:

_____
_____
_____
_____

I said a special prayer for:

_____
_____
_____
_____

Prayer(s) answered (comfort, peace, love and miracles)

_____
_____
_____

What I would like to see happen tomorrow (Goals, ideas, etc.)

_____
_____
_____
_____

MY THOUGHTS ✷ FOR THE DAY

Day: _____   *Date:* _____

The weather today:

_____
_____
_____

Today I feel:

_____
_____
_____

Today I am grateful for:

_____
_____
_____

Inspirations, prayer, scriptures, quotes:

_____
_____
_____

I said a special prayer for:

_____
_____
_____

Prayer(s) answered (comfort, peace, love and miracles)

_____
_____
_____

What I would like to see happen tomorrow (Goals, ideas, etc.)

_____
_____
_____
_____

MY THOUGHTS ✻ FOR THE DAY

Day: _____ Date: _____

The weather today:

_____
_____
_____

Today I feel:

_____
_____
_____

Today I am grateful for:

_____
_____
_____

Inspirations, prayer, scriptures, quotes:

_____
_____
_____

I said a special prayer for:

_____
_____
_____

Prayer(s) answered (comfort, peace, love and miracles)

_____
_____
_____

What I would like to see happen tomorrow (Goals, ideas, etc.)

_____
_____
_____

MY THOUGHTS ✸ FOR THE DAY

Day: _____   Date: _____

The weather today:

_____
_____
_____

Today I feel:

_____
_____
_____
_____

Today I am grateful for:

_____
_____
_____
_____

Inspirations, prayer, scriptures, quotes:

_____
_____
_____
_____

I said a special prayer for:

_____
_____
_____
_____

Prayer(s) answered (comfort, peace, love and miracles)

_____
_____
_____

What I would like to see happen tomorrow (Goals, ideas, etc.)

_____
_____
_____
_____

MY THOUGHTS ✳ FOR THE DAY

Day: _____   *Date:* _____

The weather today:

_____
_____
_____

Today I feel:

_____
_____
_____

Today I am grateful for:

_____
_____
_____

Inspirations, prayer, scriptures, quotes:

_____
_____
_____

I said a special prayer for:

_____
_____
_____

Prayer(s) answered (comfort, peace, love and miracles)

_____
_____
_____

What I would like to see happen tomorrow (Goals, ideas, etc.)

_____
_____
_____
_____

MY THOUGHTS ✳ FOR THE DAY

_____

_____

_____

_____

_____

_____

_____

_____

_____

_____

_____

_____

_____

_____

_____

_____

_____

_____

_____

_____

_____

_____

_____

_____

_____

_____

_____

_____

_____

Day: _____ *Date:* _____

The weather today:

_____
_____
_____

Today I feel:

_____
_____
_____

Today I am grateful for:

_____
_____
_____

Inspirations, prayer, scriptures, quotes:

_____
_____
_____

I said a special prayer for:

_____
_____
_____

Prayer(s) answered (comfort, peace, love and miracles)

_____
_____
_____

What I would like to see happen tomorrow (Goals, ideas, etc.)

_____
_____
_____
_____

MY THOUGHTS ✳ FOR THE DAY

Day: _____   *Date:* _____

The weather today:

_____
_____
_____

Today I feel:

_____
_____
_____

Today I am grateful for:

_____
_____
_____

Inspirations, prayer, scriptures, quotes:

_____
_____
_____

I said a special prayer for:

_____
_____
_____

Prayer(s) answered (comfort, peace, love and miracles)

_____
_____
_____

What I would like to see happen tomorrow (Goals, ideas, etc.)

_____
_____
_____
_____

MY THOUGHTS ✳ FOR THE DAY

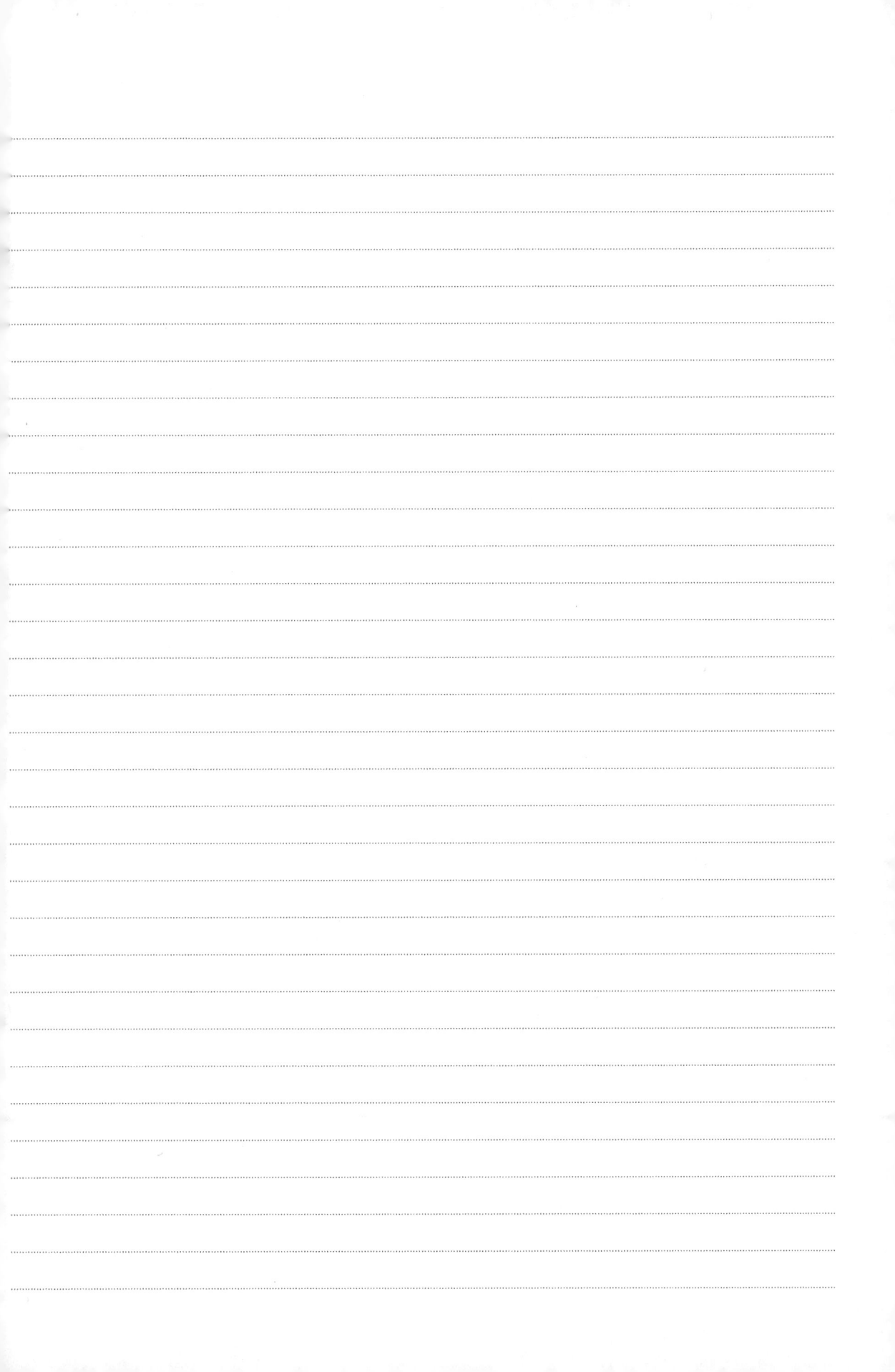

www.ingramcontent.com/pod-product-compliance
Lightning Source LLC
Chambersburg PA
CBHW081336090426

42737CB00017B/3168